The 50 Most Influential Figures in History:

History:

The Life and Legacy of the Individuals Who Shaped the World

Arthur William Gertz

"Thought is the mightiest power that exists in the universe; it is the origin of all great actions, and great actions are the origin of all great achievements." - **Swami Vivekananda**

Foreword

In this captivating historical journey, I invite you to immerse yourself in the lives and legacies of the 50 Historical Figures Who Transformed the World. Get ready to be captivated, inspired, and amazed by the most influential figures of all time.

From revolutionary visionaries to tireless leaders, brilliant scientific minds to innovative artists, this collection will take you across centuries and continents, revealing the fascinating stories of those who defied conventions and left an indelible mark on the history of humanity. As you explore their lives, you will discover the passions and sacrifices that propelled them forward, overcoming seemingly insurmountable obstacles in their quest for a better world.

Their achievements transcend time and cultures, encompassing diverse fields such as science, art, politics, philosophy, and much more.

Throughout each page, you will witness how these extraordinary men and women challenged established norms, faced adversity, and unleashed a cascade of transformation in their respective fields. Their legacy inspires us all to look beyond what is possible, to pursue our dreams with passion, and to strive for a fairer and more equitable world.

Introduction

In this book entitled "The 50 People Who Changed the World," we embark on an exciting journey through history to discover the impact of some of the most influential figures of all time. Throughout these pages, we will explore the lives and contributions of visionaries whose legacy has left an indelible mark on our society.

It is critical to recognize the importance of highlighting individual contributions to history. Often, we tend to focus on collective events and movements, forgetting that it is the actions and ideas of courageous individuals that truly drive change. These 50 characters embody that courage and determination, challenging established norms, breaking barriers and transforming the world we live in to this day.

As we explore their lives, we will discover how each of them overcame insurmountable obstacles, whether scientific, political, social or cultural. Their achievements transcended the limitations of their time and continue to inspire later generations. Through their ingenuity, passion and dedication, these celebrated individuals became true agents of change, driving progress and leaving a lasting legacy.

Jesus of Nazareth

Jesus of Nazareth is a central figure in world history and the foundation of Christianity. And considered by great and small as the most influential man of all time.

Historical context and biography:

Jesus of Nazareth was born around 4 B.C. in the region of Judea, which was part of the Roman Empire. Most of the details of his life come from the New Testament gospels of the Bible, written by his followers and other historical writings of the time. Jesus grew up in a Jewish family and lived in a society influenced by both the Jewish religion and the Roman occupation.

Key influences and experiences in his life:

Jesus was deeply influenced by the Jewish religious tradition, and it is believed that he studied the scriptures and the teachings of the prophets from childhood. At the age of thirty, he began his public ministry, preaching a message of love, forgiveness, justice and salvation throughout Israel. Jesus had a devoted following and performed numerous miracles, such as healing the sick and raising the dead.

Contributions and achievements that impacted the world:

Jesus' main contribution was the founding of Christianity, one of the most influential religions in human history. His teachings, such as love of neighbor, forgiveness and the promise of eternal life, have had a lasting impact on Western morals and ethics. Jesus also established the Christian sacraments, such as baptism and the Eucharist, which remain central to Christian religious practice to this day.

Legacy and lasting impact:

The legacy of Jesus has transcended centuries and continues to have a significant impact on Western civilization and many parts of the world. Christianity has become one of the most widespread and globally practiced religions. Its teachings on love, compassion and equality have inspired countless people throughout history, and have been central to the struggle for social justice and human rights. In addition, the figure of Jesus has been the subject of worship, theological study and artistic representation in various forms throughout the centuries.

It is important to keep in mind that, beyond religious belief, Jesus of Nazareth has had a profound cultural, philosophical and ethical impact on humanity, and his figure continues to be the subject of reflection and debate today.

Christianity is one of the largest religions in the world and has a large number of followers in different denominations. Below, I will provide a rough estimate of the total number of adherents to Christianity, taking into account both Catholics and Protestants:

Catholicism: According to the most recent statistics, the Catholic Church is the largest Christian denomination and has about 1.4 billion followers worldwide.

Protestantism: Protestantism encompasses a wide variety of denominations, including Lutherans, Baptists, Methodists, Presbyterians, Pentecostals, among others. These Protestant denominations together have approximately 800 million followers, who ultimately have a deep love for the figure of Jesus of Nazareth.

In summary, adding Catholic and Protestant followers, it is estimated that Christianity has about 2.5 billion adherents worldwide. In addition, it is estimated that, over the course of history, another two billion would have died who agreed with his teachings. For this and more, Jesus is the most influential historical figure in history.

Muhammad

Muhammad, whose full name is Muhammad Ibn Abd Allah, was born around the year 570 in Mecca, in the region of present-day Saudi Arabia. He is considered the last and foremost prophet of Islam. Muhammad received divine revelations through the angel Gabriel, which were later compiled in the Qur'an, the holy book of Islam. His life and teachings gave rise to the Islamic religion, and later, its many ramifications.

Wives and intimate life:

Muhammad had multiple wives throughout his life. It is estimated that he married around 11 to 13 women, but the exact number varies in different historical sources. Aisha, one of his wives, played an important role in the transmission of the Hadith (accounts of Muhammad's sayings and deeds) and is considered a prominent figure in Islam.

Curious facts and key experiences in his life:

During his lifetime, Muhammad faced various challenges and persecutions due to his preaching and his call to worship one God, Islam. In 622, Muhammad and his followers migrated from Mecca to Medina, an event known as the Hegira. This event marked the beginning of the Islamic calendar, and the strengthening of the Muslim community.

Contributions and achievements that impacted the world:

Muhammad laid the foundations of Islam, one of the most widespread religions in the world, with billions of followers today. His teachings encompass religious, ethical and legal aspects, and have had a profound impact on the culture, society and politics of many regions.

Legacy and lasting impact:

Muhammad's legacy is of great importance to Muslims, who consider him to be the last and most important prophet sent by God. His teaching and example are fundamental to the practice of Islam. In addition, the expansion of Islam under his leadership had a significant impact on world history, influencing political, social and cultural aspects in various regions.

The religion of Islam, founded by Muhammad in the 7th century AD, currently has approximately 1.8 billion followers worldwide. It is one of the most widespread religions and has a significant adherent base in several countries and regions of the world, especially in the Middle East, North Africa, Southeast Asia and parts of Europe.

Throughout its history, Islam has experienced steady growth and has also had periods of significant expansion. From its founding to the present, it is estimated to have had more than 4 billion people. Therefore, its impact has been significant in world history. And that is why Muhammad is the second most influential person in history.

Gautama Buddha

Gautama, also known simply as Buddha, was the founder of Buddhism and one of the most influential figures in human history.

Historical context and biography:

Gautama Buddha lived in the 6th century B.C. in the northeastern region of India, in what is now Nepal. He was born into a noble family and led a comfortable and privileged life in his youth. However, at the age of 29, he abandoned his life of wealth and luxury to embark on a spiritual quest in search of truth, and liberation from human suffering.

Intimate life and curious facts:

Gautama Buddha abandoned his family life and renounced his responsibilities as a husband and father in his spiritual quest. He spent several years practicing austerity and meditation, seeking enlightenment. During this time, he is said to have attained the state of Buddha, meaning "the enlightened one."

Key influences and experiences in his life:

The main influence on Buddha's life was his encounter with human suffering and his desire to find a solution to alleviate it. His experience of witnessing suffering, illness and death awakened in him a deep compassion and a search for truth beyond the conventional religious and philosophical teachings of his time.

Contributions and achievements that impacted the world:

Gautama Buddha founded Buddhism, a spiritual and philosophical tradition based on his teachings on human suffering and the path to liberation and enlightenment. His teachings center on the "Noble Eightfold Path," which includes practices such as right understanding, right thought, right action and meditation.

Buddha transmitted his teachings to a wide spectrum of people, from monks and nuns to kings and beggars. His message of compassion, wisdom and freedom from suffering resonated deeply with those seeking an answer to the challenges of human existence.

Legacy and lasting impact:

The Buddha's legacy is immense. His teaching of Buddhism has spread through the centuries and has influenced millions of people around the world. Buddhism has left a profound mark on global culture, philosophy and spirituality.

The Buddha's focus on compassion, nonviolence and the search for inner enlightenment has inspired numerous individuals and spawned social and philosophical movements based on his teachings. In addition, Buddhism has influenced other spiritual traditions and has promoted interfaith dialogue and the search for peace and harmony.

Global spread: Over the centuries, Buddhism has spread beyond the borders of India and has reached different parts of Asia, such as China, Japan, Tibet, Sri Lanka and Vietnam. Today, it is also practiced in various communities in the West.

Emphasis on meditation: The Buddha emphasized the practice of meditation as a means of cultivating mindfulness and deep understanding of mind and reality. His focus on meditation has influenced many contemporary traditions and approaches to meditation.

The quest for enlightenment: The central idea in Buddhism is the quest for enlightenment or spiritual awakening. Buddha taught that anyone can attain this state through understanding the Four Noble Truths and following the Noble Eightfold Path.

Ethics and morality: The Buddha's teachings also emphasize the importance of living an ethical and moral life. The concept of "karma" and the understanding of actions and their consequences are fundamental to Buddhism.

The philosophy of impermanence: The Buddha taught that everything in life is transitory and subject to change. This view of impermanence has influenced the way people perceive reality and how they deal with challenges and changes in their lives.

In summary, Gautama Buddha was a spiritual leader whose teachings have had a profound impact on spirituality, philosophy and global culture. His emphasis on compassion, wisdom and liberation from suffering has resonated throughout the centuries and continues to inspire millions of people in their quest for a meaningful and fulfilling life. It is estimated that he could exceed 500 million people today, and the number of people who have died throughout history is estimated to be another 1 billion, making him the third most influential person in history.

Albert Einstein

Albert Einstein was a German theoretical physicist of Jewish origin, born on March 14, 1879 in Ulm, Germany. His work revolutionized our understanding of time, space, gravity and energy, and he is considered one of the most influential scientists in history.

As for his personal life, Einstein married twice. His first wife was Mileva Marić, with whom he had three children, and his second wife was Elsa Löwenthal. As for his intimate life and specific details about his sexuality, detailed records are not available, and Einstein maintained strict privacy in these matters.

Some curious facts about Einstein include his passion for playing the violin and his love of sailing. He is also said to have had messy hair and is often credited with the phrase "Imagination is more important than knowledge."

Key influences and experiences in Einstein's life included the study of physics at the University of Zurich, where he graduated in 1900. During his time at the Swiss Patent Office, he published several groundbreaking scientific papers, including the famous paper on the theory of special relativity in 1905.

Einstein's contributions and achievements that impacted the world are numerous. His theory of special relativity and his famous equation $E = mc^2$ changed our understanding of the relationship between energy and mass, and laid the foundation for the development of modern physics. His theory of general relativity, published in 1915, provided a new description of gravity and predicted the existence of black holes.

Einstein's legacy and lasting impact are enormous. His ideas and discoveries have transformed our understanding of the universe and have had practical applications in fields such as satellite technology, nuclear energy and cosmology. In addition, Einstein was an advocate of pacifism and fought for equality and civil rights. His influence goes beyond science, being a symbol of genius and creativity that inspires generations of scientists and thinkers.

Abraham Lincoln

Was the sixteenth president of the United States, born on February 12, 1809 in Hodgenville, Kentucky. His presidential term took place during a crucial period in American history: the Civil War (1861-1865) and the abolition of slavery.

As for his personal life, Lincoln married Mary Todd in 1842 and they had four children together. As for his intimate life and details about his sexuality, there are no records available to indicate that Lincoln had romantic or sexual relationships with persons of the same sex, although there has been some speculation and theories about this.

A curious fact about Lincoln is that he was known for his height, as he was about 1.93 meters tall. He was also a skilled orator and is credited with the most famous speech of his political career, the Gettysburg Address.

Key influences and experiences in Lincoln's life include his humble upbringing in a farming family, his self-education, and his involvement in politics. Before becoming president, Lincoln practiced law and became involved in Illinois state politics.

Lincoln's contributions and accomplishments that impacted the world are significant. As president, he led the United States through the Civil War and played a crucial role in preserving the Union and abolishing slavery. He is remembered for his Emancipation Proclamation of 1863, which declared freedom for slaves in the rebellious states, laying the groundwork for the total abolition of slavery in the United States.

Lincoln's legacy and lasting impact are vast. His leadership during the Civil War and his fight for racial equality and justice have been central to the history of the United States. His image and ideals have become symbols of freedom and democracy. In addition, his assassination in 1865 made him a national martyr and contributed to his veneration as one of the most prominent presidents in U.S. history.

Leonardo da Vinci

Leonardo was a leading Italian polymath of the Renaissance, known for his skills in painting, sculpture, architecture, music, anatomy and engineering.

Historical context and biography:
Leonardo da Vinci was born on April 15, 1452 in Vinci, Italy. He lived in an era of great artistic and scientific effervescence, known as the Renaissance. Da Vinci apprenticed in the workshop of the painter Andrea del Verrocchio and developed his own artistic style characterized by realism, depth and technical mastery.

Intimate life and curious facts:
There is no record that Leonardo da Vinci ever had a wife or children. Although few details are known about his intimate life, it is believed that he was homosexual, based on some of his writings and personal drawings. In addition to his outstanding artistic ability, he also devoted himself to anatomy and made numerous detailed studies of the human body.

Key influences and experiences in his life:
Da Vinci was influenced by the cultural milieu of the Italian Renaissance, as well as by leading figures of his time, including painters Andrea del Verrocchio and Sandro Botticelli. In addition, his curiosity and inquisitive mind led him to study a wide variety of disciplines, from anatomy to engineering to astronomy.

Contributions and achievements that impacted the world:
Leonardo da Vinci left an impressive legacy in both the artistic and scientific fields. His most famous paintings, such as "The Last Supper" and "The Mona Lisa," have left an enduring mark on the history of art.

His works displayed unprecedented technical mastery and an innovative approach to the use of perspective and the depiction of the human figure.

In addition to his artistic contribution, da Vinci made numerous discoveries and designs in fields such as anatomy, physics, engineering and architecture. His notebooks contain a wealth of sketches and innovative ideas, from designs for flying machines to detailed studies of human anatomy.

Legacy and lasting impact:

Leonardo da Vinci's legacy is undeniable in the history of art and science. His multidisciplinary approach and his ability to combine artistic creativity with scientific observation laid the foundation for the Renaissance and for later advances in fields such as anatomy, engineering and astronomy.

His interdisciplinary vision and insatiable curiosity continue to be a source of inspiration for artists and scientists today. Da Vinci demonstrated the importance of combining creativity with scientific knowledge to achieve significant advances in different fields.

Mahatma Gandhi

He was an Indian political and spiritual leader, known for his role in the struggle for India's independence and his advocacy of non-violence.

Historical context and biography:

Mohandas Karamchand Gandhi was born on October 2, 1869 in Porbandar, a city in the state of Gujarat, India. Gandhi grew up in a Hindu family and was educated in law in London. After returning to India, Gandhi became a political leader and civil rights advocate, leading nonviolent movements and campaigns for India's independence from British rule.

Wife and intimate life:

Gandhi married Kasturba Makhanji at the age of 13 in an arranged marriage. Kasturba was a loyal companion to Gandhi and also became a civil rights activist. They had four children together, but their family life was marked by the demands of political struggle and community life.

Key influences and experiences in his life:

Gandhi was influenced by various philosophies and religions, including Hinduism, Jainism, Christianity and the teachings of figures such as Henry David Thoreau and Leo Tolstoy. The racial discrimination he experienced in South Africa and his encounter with the civil rights movement in that country were key experiences that led him to develop his philosophy of nonviolent resistance and civil disobedience.

Contributions and achievements that impacted the world:

Gandhi is known for his leadership in the struggle for India's independence using nonviolent resistance tactics. His philosophy of "Satyagraha" (steadfastness in truth) became a powerful method of fighting injustice and oppression. Gandhi organized civil disobedience campaigns, boycotts of British goods and hunger strikes to promote freedom and civil rights.

Legacy and lasting impact:

Gandhi's legacy has left a profound mark on world history and politics. His focus on nonviolence and peaceful resistance has influenced leaders and movements around the world, such as Martin Luther King Jr. and Nelson Mandela. Gandhi also advocated social equality, economic justice and religious harmony. His vision of an independent and united India became a reality in 1947, when the country achieved independence.

Gandhi's legacy transcends his role in India's independence. His philosophy and methods of nonviolence continue to inspire the struggle for human rights, social justice and peace around the world. Gandhi is internationally recognized as an icon of peaceful resistance and his message of love, tolerance and compassion continues to resonate today.

In addition, Gandhi advocated gender equality and the emancipation of women, fighting for their full participation in society. He also advocated environmental protection and sustainability, recognizing the interconnectedness between humans and nature.

In summary, Mahatma Gandhi left a significant legacy in history by leading the peaceful struggle for India's independence and promoting nonviolence as an effective form of resistance against unequal and tyrannical systems. His message of love, tolerance, social justice and peaceful resistance remains relevant and his figure is admired as a symbol of the struggle for freedom and peace throughout the world.

Martin Luther King Jr.

He was a prominent leader of the civil rights movement in the United States.

Historical context and biography:

Martin Luther King Jr. was born on January 15, 1929 in Atlanta, Georgia, during a period of racial segregation and discrimination in the United States. He was a Baptist pastor and became a prominent civil rights advocate, leading numerous peaceful protests to combat injustice and racial segregation.

Intimate life and curious facts:

Martin Luther King Jr. married Coretta Scott King in 1953, and they had four children together. Although he is known primarily for his leadership in the civil rights movement, he was also a devoted father and committed husband.

Key influences and experiences in his life:

King's childhood and upbringing in the segregated U.S. South, as well as the teachings of his father and mother, influenced his vision of equality and justice. He was also influenced by the activism of figures such as Mahatma Gandhi and Henry David Thoreau, who promoted peaceful resistance and civil disobedience as means for social change.

Contributions and achievements that impacted the world:

Martin Luther King Jr. was the foremost leader of the civil rights movement in the United States. His famous "I Have a Dream" speech during the 1963 March on Washington became a symbol of the struggle for racial equality and justice. His nonviolent struggle and advocacy for civil rights inspired millions of people and were instrumental in the passage of important legislation such as the Civil Rights Act of 1964 and the Voting Rights Act of 1965.

Legacy and lasting impact:

Martin Luther King Jr.'s legacy lives on in the struggle for equality and justice around the world. His courage and peaceful leadership have been a source of inspiration for social movements and leaders in diverse causes. His focus on nonviolence, justice and brotherly love continues to resonate in the struggle for human rights.

In addition, King also advocated for the elimination of poverty and the promotion of economic equality, and his message about the interconnectedness of struggles for race, class and social justice remains relevant today.

In summary, Martin Luther King Jr. was a charismatic leader and pacifist whose commitment to racial equality and social justice had a significant impact on the struggle for civil rights in the United States. His legacy of nonviolent resistance and his vision of a more just world continue to inspire today's generations in their quest for equality and justice.

Confucius

Whose real name was Kong Qiu, was a Chinese philosopher and educator who lived during the Zhou Dynasty period in the 5th century BC.

Historical context and biography:

Confucius was born in 551 BC in the city of Qufu, in present-day Shandong Province, China. He lived during a time of political and social turmoil, known as the Period of the Warring Kingdoms, characterized by war and political fragmentation. Confucius strove to restore social harmony and promote stability through ethics and education.

Intimate life and curious facts:

Little is known about Confucius' intimate life. He married and had several children, but no specific details are known about his family or romantic life. Confucius focused on his studies and his mission to transmit his teachings to his disciples and future generations.

Key influences and experiences in his life:

Confucius was influenced by ancient Chinese traditions and philosophies, such as Confucianism and Taoism. He also studied and was inspired by the social and political practices of the time, seeking ways to improve society through morality and righteousness.

Contributions and achievements that impacted the world:

Confucius' teachings, compiled in the book known as "Analects", focus on ethics, morality and personal virtue. He advocated the importance of harmonious family relationships, loyalty to the government and respect for elders. His influence on education and moral formation has endured for centuries in Chinese culture.

Legacy and lasting impact:

Confucius' legacy has had a significant impact on Chinese society and many other East Asian cultures. His teachings became the basis of Confucianism, a philosophy that influenced politics, morality and education in China for centuries. His ideas on social harmony, virtue and ethics continue to be studied and debated today.

In addition, Confucius' teachings have also influenced the formation of educational systems and the promotion of moral values in various societies. His emphasis on righteousness, respect and wisdom has left a lasting imprint on thought and culture throughout the world.

Winston Churchill

He was a British politician and leader during World War II.

Historical context and biography:

Winston Churchill was born on November 30, 1874 in Woodstock, Oxfordshire, United Kingdom. He lived at a time of major geopolitical change, including the rise of British imperialism and the political challenges of the two world wars. Churchill held various political positions throughout his life, including Prime Minister of the United Kingdom on two occasions.

Intimate life and curious facts:

Churchill married Clementine Hozier in 1908, and they had five children together. Although there are few details about his intimate life, it is known that Churchill was a prolific writer and an avid painter. In addition, Churchill was known for his passion for cigars and his taste for whiskey.

Key influences and experiences in his life:

Churchill grew up in a political environment, as his father was also a politician. His experiences in the army and his participation in World War I gave him a unique insight into the challenges and dangers of war. He was also influenced by history and literature, and acquired a deep understanding of politics and strategy.

Contributions and achievements that impacted the world:

During World War II, Churchill was a key figure in the British resistance against Nazi Germany. His inspirational speeches and steadfast leadership gave hope to the British people in difficult times. In addition, Churchill played a crucial role in the formation of the Allied coalition and in the strategic planning for the war.

Legacy and lasting impact:

Churchill's legacy lies in his leadership during World War II and his role in the defense of democratic values. His speeches and determination have left a lasting impression on history. Churchill was also noted for his geopolitical vision and his advocacy of international cooperation, which contributed to the formation of organizations such as the United Nations.

In addition, Churchill was awarded the Nobel Prize for Literature in 1953 for his mastery of oratory and historical writing. His literary works, such as "The Second World War" and "History of the English-Speaking Peoples," have been widely read and studied. In summary, Winston Churchill was an outstanding British political leader whose leadership during World War II and his contributions to the defense of democratic values left a lasting legacy. His steadfastness, inspirational oratory and commitment to peace and international cooperation remain relevant examples today.

Alexander the Great

Also known as Alexander III of Macedon, was a prominent military and political leader who lived in the 4th century BC.

Historical context and biography:

Alexander the Great was born on July 20, 356 BC in Pella, Macedonia. He was the son of King Philip II of Macedon and inherited the throne at the age of 20, following the assassination of his father. His reign was marked by a series of military campaigns that led to the expansion of the Macedonian Empire into Asia, reaching as far as Egypt and India.

Intimate life and curious facts:

As for his intimate life, Alexander the Great was married three times. His first wife was Roxana, a Bactrian princess, with whom he had a son named Alexander IV. Intimate relations with men are also attributed to him, which was common in the Macedonian culture of the time.

Key influences and experiences in his life:

The greatest influence in the life of Alexander the Great was his father, Philip II, who educated him in the arts, philosophy and warfare. He also received teachings from the famous Greek philosopher Aristotle. These influences provided him with a well-rounded education and helped him develop skills in leadership, military strategy and political thinking.

Contributions and achievements that impacted the world:

Alexander the Great's greatest achievement was the creation of one of the greatest empires in history. His bold military campaign conquered much of the known world in his time, from Greece and Egypt to Persia, India and beyond. His innovative military tactics and his ability to unite his troops made him one of the most successful military leaders in history.

Legacy and lasting impact:

Alexander the Great's legacy was significant both politically and culturally. His conquest spread Hellenistic Greek culture throughout his empire, influencing the architecture, art and literature of the conquered regions. In addition, his political legacy laid the foundation for the rise of the Hellenistic kingdoms after his death.

Alexander the Great is also remembered as a visionary leader who sought the unification of different cultures and the spread of knowledge. He founded numerous cities, many of which bore his name, such as Alexandria in Egypt, which became an important cultural and commercial center.

Aristotle

He was a Greek philosopher and scientist who lived in the 4th century BC.

Historical context and biography:

Aristotle was born in 384 BC in the city of Stagira, in ancient Macedonia. He was a disciple of Plato and later became a tutor to the young Alexander the Great. He developed his teachings and wrote extensively on a wide range of subjects, including philosophy, ethics, politics, logic, biology and physics.

Intimate life and curious facts:

As for his intimate life, Aristotle was married twice. His first wife was Pythias, with whom he had a daughter named Pythias. After he was widowed, he married a woman named Herpyllis, with whom he had a son named Nicomachus. In addition, Aristotle is known to have founded his own school, the Lyceum, where he taught and conducted research.

Key influences and experiences in his life:

Aristotle was greatly influenced by his teacher, Plato, who in turn was a disciple of Socrates. Aristotle's philosophy was based on the thinking of these two great philosophers. In addition, his time as tutor to Alexander the Great allowed him to gain experiences in politics and leadership, which influenced his ideas on the organization of society.

Contributions and achievements that impacted the world:

Aristotle's contributions are vast and cover diverse fields of knowledge. He was one of the first to develop a formal logical system and his work "Organon" laid the foundations of classical logic. His writings on ethics and politics, such as "Nicomachean Ethics" and "Politics", continue to be important references in these fields.

In the field of natural sciences, Aristotle conducted detailed investigations and classifications in areas such as biology and zoology. His works, such as "History of Animals" and "De Anima", laid the foundations for the systematic study of life and mind.

Legacy and lasting impact:

Aristotle's legacy is immense and has endured throughout the centuries. His teachings and writings have been continuously studied and debated, influencing fields such as philosophy, ethics, politics, logic and the natural sciences. His logical and systematic approach has had a lasting impact on Western thought and has laid the foundations for many academic disciplines.

In addition, Aristotle founded the Lyceum, which became an important center of study and teaching. His disciples, known as peripatetics, continued his legacy and spread his ideas.

Aristotle also established the method of systematic observation and classification in the study of nature, laying the foundation for subsequent scientific research. His contributions in biology, zoology and other scientific areas have left a lasting mark on the understanding of the natural world.

Isaac Newton

(1643-1727) was an outstanding English scientist, mathematician and physicist who made fundamental contributions in the fields of physics, mathematics and astronomy.

Historical context:

Isaac Newton lived in an era known as the Age of Enlightenment and the Scientific Renaissance. He was born on 25 December 1643 in Woolsthorpe, England, during the reign of Charles I. His life and work unfolded at a time of great intellectual and scientific change.

Biography:

Newton grew up on a farm and showed a great talent for mathematics from a young age. He studied at Cambridge University and became a professor at Trinity College. During his lifetime, Newton never married and is considered a bachelor.

Intimate life:

Newton's personal life has been the subject of speculation and debate. It is known that he was an introverted person and obsessed with his scientific work. He spent long hours immersed in his research and experiments, which led him to neglect other areas of his life.

Curious facts:

Newton experienced a nervous breakdown in his youth and withdrew from public life for a period.

He was known for his difficult personality and conflicts with other scientists of the time, such as Robert Hooke and Gottfried Leibniz.

Newton was a member of the British Parliament for a brief period.

In addition to his scientific contributions, Newton was also interested in alchemy and theology.

Key influences and experiences:

Newton was influenced by the work of earlier scientists, such as Galileo Galilei, Johannes Kepler and René Descartes. These influences led him to develop his famous theory of universal gravitation and the laws of motion, which revolutionized physics.

Contributions and achievements:

He formulated the laws of motion, known as Newton's Laws, which are fundamental to classical physics.

He developed the theory of universal gravitation, explaining the attraction between celestial bodies.

He made important advances in mathematics, especially in differential and integral calculus.

He was the first to decompose white light into a spectrum of colors by means of a prism, laying the foundations of modern optics.

Legacy and lasting impact:

Isaac Newton's legacy is undeniable. His discoveries laid the foundations of modern physics and transformed our understanding of the natural world. His scientific approach based on observation, experimentation and logical reasoning laid the foundations of the scientific method and has influenced generations of scientists ever since. His ideas and theories continue to be fundamental in many fields of science and his name is associated with genius and scientific revolution.

Louis Pasteur

Born December 27, 1822 in Dole, France, and died September 28, 1895 in Marnes-la-Coquette, he was a scientist and chemist noted for his contributions to microbiology and medicine.

As for his personal life, Pasteur married Marie Laurent in 1849, with whom he had five children. In terms of his intimate life, not many details are available, as it is not a widely documented aspect.

Pasteur lived in a historical context in which medicine and science were undergoing rapid development. He was influenced by the discovery of germ theory and the idea that microorganisms were the cause of many diseases. His key experiences included his work on fermentation, vaccination and sterilization.

His most outstanding contributions and achievements include the development of the pasteurization technique, which allowed the preservation of food and the prevention of diseases transmitted by contaminated food. He also developed vaccines for diseases such as rabies and anthrax, laying the foundations for modern immunization.

Louis Pasteur's legacy is of great importance in the field of medicine and microbiology. His discoveries revolutionized the understanding of infectious diseases and laid the foundation for the development of modern microbiology. His rigorous scientific approach and contributions to medicine have saved countless lives and have had a lasting impact on public health.

In addition, Pasteur was one of the first scientists to recognize the importance of scientific dissemination and the practical application of scientific discoveries for the benefit of society. His work and dedication to science have left a lasting legacy and have laid the foundation for scientific and medical advancement throughout the world.

Nelson Mandela

He was a South African leader and an emblematic figure in the struggle against apartheid.

Historical context and biography:

Nelson Mandela was born on July 18, 1918 in Mvezo, South Africa. He lived at a time when South Africa was marked by racial discrimination and the policy of apartheid, a system of institutionalized racial segregation. Mandela became a tireless advocate for equality and justice for all South Africans, regardless of race.

Intimate life and curious facts:

Nelson Mandela was married three times. His first wife was Evelyn Mase, with whom he had four children. Later, he married Winnie Madikizela, with whom he had two daughters. His third marriage was to Graça Machel, widow of the former president of Mozambique, Samora Machel. Mandela was a father, grandfather and great-grandfather, and his family played an important role in his struggle and legacy.

Key influences and experiences in his life:

Mandela's experience growing up in a segregated South Africa and his encounter with racial discrimination influenced his commitment to the struggle for equality. His experience as leader of the African National Congress (ANC), his imprisonment for 27 years and his relationship with other political leaders and civil rights activists were key experiences that shaped his determination and his vision of a free and democratic South Africa.

Contributions and achievements that impacted the world:

Nelson Mandela's most outstanding contribution was his leadership in the struggle against apartheid and his role in South Africa's peaceful transition to democracy. After his release from prison in 1990, Mandela played a crucial role in the negotiations to end apartheid and became South Africa's first black president in 1994.

Legacy and lasting impact:

Nelson Mandela's legacy is characterized by his tireless struggle for justice and equality. His leadership inspired people around the world and he became a symbol of peaceful resistance and reconciliation. His focus on national reconciliation and the promotion of unity and racial equality helped avert a civil war and laid the foundation for the building of a democratic and multicultural South Africa.

Mandela received numerous international awards and recognitions, including the Nobel Peace Prize in 1993, in recognition of his contribution to the peaceful resolution of the conflict in South Africa. His legacy continues to inspire leaders and activists around the world in the struggle for social justice and human rights.

Socrates

He was a Greek philosopher who lived in Athens during the 5th century BC.

Historical context and biography:

Socrates was born around 470 BC in Athens, Greece, during a period of cultural and political flourishing known as the Golden Age of Athens. Although he left no written records, his philosophy and teachings were transmitted through the writings of his disciples, especially Plato.

Intimate life and curious facts:

As for his intimate life, Socrates was married to Jantipa and had three children with her. It is said that their marriage was unconventional and that Jantipa was a temperamental woman. In addition, Socrates had close and lasting relationships with several of his disciples, including Plato.

Curious facts about Socrates include his teaching style, known as the "Socratic method," which was based on asking questions and challenging established beliefs. He is also credited with the phrase "I only know that I know nothing," which reflects his intellectual humility and constant quest for knowledge.

Key influences and experiences in his life:

Socrates was influenced by various thinkers and philosophical currents of his time, such as the Sophists and the philosophy of Heraclitus and Parmenides. However, it was his encounter with the Oracle of Delphi and his interpretation of its message, which designated him as the wisest man in Athens, that led him to question established beliefs and knowledge.

Contributions and achievements that impacted the world:

Socrates left no written works, but his method of inquiry and his focus on the search for truth and knowledge had a significant impact on Western philosophy. His teaching style and his insistence on examining beliefs and questioning assumptions laid the foundation for critical thinking and systematic philosophy.

In addition, Socrates was an advocate of ethics and virtue. He believed in the importance of self-reflection and self-discipline in achieving moral excellence. His discussions on justice, virtue and the nature of the human being influenced generations of later philosophers.

Legacy and lasting impact:

Socrates' legacy lies in his focus on the search for truth and virtue, as well as his method of inquiry. Although he was condemned to death for "corrupting the youth" and "not recognizing the gods of the city," his figure and teachings have endured through the centuries.

Socrates laid the foundation for the development of Western philosophy and has been an influential figure in philosophical thought to this day. His teachings and method of inquiry have been studied and discussed by philosophers throughout the centuries, and his focus on self-knowledge, ethics and the search for truth continues to be relevant in contemporary philosophy.

Galileo Galilei

He was an Italian scientist who lived during the sixteenth and seventeenth centuries.

Historical context and biography:

Galileo Galilei was born on February 15, 1564 in Pisa, Italy, in an era known as the Renaissance. He was a contemporary of great figures such as Leonardo da Vinci and Michelangelo. Galileo excelled as an astronomer, physicist and mathematician, and is considered one of the fathers of modern science.

Intimate life and curious facts:

As for his intimate life, Galileo was celibate and devoted himself entirely to his studies and scientific career. However, he had three illegitimate children with Marina Gamba, a Venetian woman with whom he maintained a relationship for many years.

Curious facts about Galileo include his invention of the astronomical telescope, with which he made important observations of the sky and discovered phenomena such as the moons of Jupiter. He is also credited with formulating the law of falling bodies and the study of kinematics.

Key influences and experiences in his life:

Galileo was influenced by the natural philosophy of ancient Greece, especially by the ideas of Archimedes and Copernicus. His studies and observations in astronomy and physics led him to challenge traditional beliefs and question the geocentric system, which held that the Earth was at the center of the universe.

Contributions and achievements that impacted the world:

Galileo made numerous discoveries and significant contributions to science. His astronomical observations supported Copernicus' heliocentric theory, which stated that the planets revolve around the

Sun. His defense of this theory and his confrontation with the Catholic Church led him to be tried for heresy and sentenced to house arrest for the rest of his life.

Galileo also laid the foundations of the modern scientific method by promoting experimentation, observation and the formulation of hypotheses as tools for understanding the natural world. His approach to the application of mathematics to physics was also revolutionary and opened new doors for the study of natural phenomena.

Legacy and lasting impact:

Galileo's legacy lies in his contribution to the scientific revolution and in his defense of freedom of thought and the autonomy of science. His struggle to establish the primacy of scientific evidence and empirical observation laid the foundations for modern scientific thought and has had a lasting impact on the development of science and society.

His contributions include perfecting the telescope, observing the phases of Venus and the moons of Jupiter, and formulating the law of falling bodies. In addition, his approach to the scientific method, based on experimentation and observation, laid the foundations of modern science and had a lasting impact on the development of disciplines such as physics and astronomy.

Galileo's legacy extends beyond his scientific discoveries. His defense of the autonomy of science and his struggle for intellectual freedom laid the foundation for modern scientific thought and the separation of religion and science. His courage and perseverance have inspired later generations of scientists and advocates of reason and evidence-based knowledge.

Henry Ford

Born July 30, 1863 in Wayne County, Michigan, and died April 7, 1947 in Dearborn, Michigan, he was a businessman and pioneer of the American automobile industry.

As for his personal life, Ford married Clara Ford in 1888, with whom he had a son named Edsel Ford. In terms of his intimate life, not many details are available, as it is not a widely documented aspect.

Ford lived in a historical context in which industry and technology were experiencing rapid growth. He was influenced by the development of automotive technology and the growing demand for personal transportation. He experimented with different ideas and approaches to improve automobile production.

His most outstanding contributions and achievements center on the automotive industry. Ford was the founder of Ford Motor Company in 1903 and is credited with introducing the assembly line to the mass production of automobiles. His popular automobile model, the Ford T, revolutionized the industry and became the first automobile accessible to the American working class.

Henry Ford's legacy extends beyond the automotive industry. His focus on efficient, mass production laid the foundation for mass production in a variety of industries. In addition, his vision of making automobiles affordable for the masses transformed mobility and changed the way people got around.

However, Ford has also come under fire for his controversial positions and actions, such as his anti-Semitism and support for questionable political and social movements.

In short, Henry Ford was a visionary entrepreneur who revolutionized the automotive industry and left a lasting impact on mass production and mobility. His legacy is found in both business and society, although he is also remembered for his controversial opinions and actions.

William Shakespeare

He was a renowned English playwright and poet who lived during the sixteenth and early seventeenth centuries.

Historical context and biography:

Shakespeare was born in Stratford-upon-Avon, England, in 1564. His era, known as the English Renaissance, was a period of cultural and artistic flourishing in England. Shakespeare lived during the reign of Queen Elizabeth I and the subsequent reign of King James I. He was a contemporary of figures such as Francis Bacon and Miguel de Cervantes.

Intimate life and curious facts:

Shakespeare married Anne Hathaway in 1582, and they had three children together. However, very little is known about his intimate life and specific details about his relationship with his wife.

As for fun facts, Shakespeare wrote around 39 plays, including tragedies, comedies, histories and sonnets. In addition, it is believed that he invented about 1,700 English words, many of which are still used today.

Key influences and experiences in his life:

Shakespeare's influences were varied and included both classical literature, such as the works of Plutarch and Ovid, as well as the popular theatrical traditions of his time. His experience as an actor and playwright in the Lord Chamberlain's Men theater company also influenced his writing style and his understanding of drama.

Contributions and achievements that impacted the world:

Shakespeare's plays have had a significant impact on literature and theater worldwide. His plays explore a wide range of universal themes such as love, betrayal, ambition and human nature. His complex characters and poetic dialogue have been the subject of study and admiration throughout the centuries.

Some of his best-known plays include "Romeo and Juliet," "Hamlet," "Macbeth," "Othello," and "A Midsummer Night's Dream." His ability to capture human emotions and conflicts in his plays makes him one of the most important playwrights of all time.

Legacy and lasting impact:

Shakespeare's legacy endures to this day. His plays continue to be performed in theaters around the world and have been adapted to various art forms, such as film and television. His characters and iconic phrases have left an indelible mark on popular culture. In addition, Shakespeare has influenced numerous later writers and artists. His literary style, mastery of language and exploration of universal themes have inspired generations of writers and left an indelible mark on literature and theater.

Thomas Edison

Born February 11, 1847 in Milan, Ohio, and died October 18, 1931 in West Orange, New Jersey, he was an American inventor and entrepreneur known for his numerous inventions and contributions to the field of electricity and lighting.

As for his personal life, Edison married twice. His first wife was Mary Stilwell, with whom he had three children, but unfortunately, she died in 1884. Later, Edison married Mina Miller, with whom he had three more children.

Edison lived in a historical context marked by the Industrial Revolution and technological advances. His interest in science and experimentation was manifested from an early age. During his lifetime, Edison obtained more than a thousand patents, making him one of the most prolific inventors in history.

Among his most notable inventions were the incandescent lamp, the phonograph and the direct current electric power distribution system. These inventions had a significant impact on the world by improving household lighting, revolutionizing the music industry and providing a more efficient and affordable source of energy.

Thomas Edison's legacy is manifested in the way electricity and lighting have transformed our lives. His contributions laid the foundation for the development of the electrical industry and modern technology. In addition, Edison established the concept of research and development laboratories, setting a model for technological innovation.

It is important to mention that Edison's figure has also been the subject of debate and controversy. Some of his business practices and his relationship with other inventors have been questioned. Likewise, the role of other inventors, such as Nikola Tesla, in the development of certain inventions attributed to Edison has been discussed.

In summary, Thomas Edison was an inventor and entrepreneur whose inventions in the field of electricity and lighting have had a lasting impact on the world. His legacy lies in the way electricity has transformed modern society. While his figure is recognized, his role and some of his practices have also been debated and discussed.

Napoleon Bonaparte

He was a prominent French military and political leader who played a crucial role in European history.

Historical context and biography:

Napoleon Bonaparte was born on August 15, 1769 in Corsica, a Mediterranean island that was then part of the Kingdom of France. In his youth, he excelled in military education and joined the French army during the French Revolution. Taking advantage of the opportunities that arose during this period of political and military upheaval, Napoleon quickly rose through the ranks of the army and became a prominent leader.

Intimate life and curious facts:

Napoleon married on several occasions. His most famous wife was Josephine de Beauharnais, whom he married in 1796. However, their marriage faced difficulties and they finally divorced in 1809. Napoleon then married Marie Louise of Austria in 1810 and had a son with her, who became the King of Rome.

Key influences and experiences in his life:

Napoleon was influenced by the ideas of the French Revolution and became an advocate of republicanism. His military career and his victories on the battlefield brought him fame and power. His experience in warfare provided him with strategic and tactical skills that allowed him to expand his empire and exert political dominance over much of Europe.

Contributions and achievements that impacted the world:

Napoleon made numerous significant contributions and achievements during his rule. Some of the most notable include:

The Napoleonic Code: Introduced a unified and modern legal system known as the Napoleonic Civil Code, which laid the foundation for modern legal systems in many countries.

Expansion of the French Empire: Napoleon led a series of successful military campaigns that led to the expansion of the French Empire and the incorporation of several territories under his rule.

Modernization of the administration: Implemented administrative reforms in France and in the conquered territories, improving the efficiency and centralization of government.

Promotion of education and culture: He promoted public education, founded numerous schools and academies, and supported the arts and sciences.

Legacy and lasting impact:

Napoleon's legacy is complex and controversial. On the one hand, his conquests and reforms modernized and transformed Europe in many respects. However, his imperial ambition and authoritarian leadership style also led to massive wars and conflicts that caused human suffering and the loss of countless lives.

Charles Darwin

He was a leading English scientist known for his revolutionary contributions to the field of biology and the theory of evolution.

Historical context and biography:

Charles Darwin was born on February 12, 1809 in England. He lived in a time of great scientific and social advancement, known as the Victorian Era. He studied medicine and theology, but his passion for natural history led him to embark on a voyage of exploration on the HMS Beagle. During this five-year voyage around the world, Darwin made observations and collected data that would lay the foundation for his ideas on evolution.

Intimate life and curious facts:

Charles Darwin married Emma Wedgwood in 1839, and together they had ten children. Darwin was known to be a dedicated family man and cared deeply for the welfare of his wife and children. In addition, he suffered from chronic health problems, and spent much of his life dealing with various ailments.

Key influences and experiences in his life:

The main influence on Darwin's life was his voyage aboard the HMS Beagle. During this expedition, he visited various regions of the world, observed the diversity of species and became interested in geology and natural history. The observations he made during the voyage and subsequent studies based on his findings were fundamental to the development of his theory of evolution.

Contributions and achievements that impacted the world:

Darwin's most outstanding achievement was the formulation of the theory of evolution through natural selection. His most influential work, "The Origin of Species," published in 1859, presented his theory that all species evolve over time through a process of natural selection, where organisms with advantageous characteristics are more likely to survive and reproduce.

Legacy and lasting impact:

Darwin's theory of evolution had a significant impact on science and the understanding of life on Earth. His work challenged traditional ideas about divine creation and laid the foundation for modern biology. Darwinism, as his theory is commonly known, has influenced a wide range of disciplines, including biology, genetics, anthropology, and evolutionary psychology. Darwin's legacy has also had implications in the social and cultural realm. It has generated debates about the relationship between science and religion, as well as ethical and moral issues related to life and species diversity. His focus on scientific evidence, observation and experimentation has set an important precedent for scientific research in general.

Adolf Hitler

He was a German politician who led the Nazi party and played a central role in the initiation and development of World War II. Although I can provide information about his historical context, biography and some aspects of his personal life, it is important to note that discussing his intimate life and fun facts may be offensive due to the horrific crimes and atrocities committed during his regime. Therefore, I will focus on providing objective facts about his life and legacy:

Historical context and biography:

Adolf Hitler was born on April 20, 1889 in Braunau am Inn, Austria. He moved to Germany as a young man and joined the German Workers' Party, which would later become the National Socialist German Workers' (Nazi) Party. Hitler became the party's leader in 1920 and quickly consolidated his power and leadership in Germany at the time.

Intimate life and curious facts:

Hitler was briefly married to Eva Braun, who was his romantic partner for several years. The couple married in a bunker in Berlin on April 29, 1945, shortly before they both committed suicide. As for fun facts, it is important to keep in mind that discussing trivial aspects of Hitler's life can minimize the gravity of his actions and the suffering caused by his regime.

Key influences and experiences in his life:

Hitler was deeply influenced by anti-Semitic ideology, extreme nationalism and social Darwinism, among other elements. His time in Vienna, where he became interested in politics and radical ideas, as well as his experience during World War I, influenced his worldview and his desire to restore Germany to greatness.

Contributions and achievements that impacted the world:

Hitler's impact on the world was devastating. Under his leadership, Germany unleashed World War II, which resulted in the deaths of millions of people and the mass destruction of cities and nations. In addition, Hitler was responsible for the Holocaust, the systematic genocide and persecution of millions of Jews and other groups deemed "undesirable" by the Nazi regime.

Legacy and lasting impact:

Hitler's legacy is one of the darkest episodes in modern history. His Nazi regime and its racist and totalitarian policies left an indelible mark on the world. The atrocities committed during his rule serve as a grim reminder of the dangers of bigotry, intolerance and abuse of power. The Holocaust and World War II have had a lasting impact on global consciousness and have led to an increased focus on human rights and the prevention of atrocities in today's world.

Mao Zedong

He was a Chinese political leader and revolutionary who played a pivotal role in the founding of the People's Republic of China and the formation of its communist government. Below, I will provide you with information about his historical context and biography, some key influences on his life, his contributions and achievements, as well as his legacy and lasting impact. However, please note that discussing his intimate life and trivial aspects may be limited due to the availability of information and the complexity of his regime:

Historical context and biography:

Mao Zedong was born on December 26, 1893 in Shaoshan, China. He lived at a time of great political and social turmoil, marked by the fall of the Qing dynasty and the struggle for power in China. Mao became involved early in revolutionary activities and became one of the leaders of the Communist Party of China.

Intimate life and curious facts:

Mao Zedong married several times during his lifetime. His best known wife was Jiang Qing, who also played a prominent role during the Cultural Revolution. As for fun facts, it is known that Mao was an avid swimmer and enjoyed poetry and reading.

Key influences and experiences in his life:

Mao Zedong was influenced by a variety of ideas and experiences throughout his life. He was inspired by communism and the class struggle promoted by Karl Marx, as well as the revolutionary theories of Vladimir Lenin. In addition, Mao's experiences during the revolutionary struggle and the Chinese Civil War shaped his ideology and political approach.

Contributions and achievements that impacted the world:

Mao Zedong led the Chinese Revolution and established the People's Republic of China in 1949. Under his leadership, radical policies such as agricultural collectivization and accelerated industrialization were implemented. However, he was also associated with the Great Chinese Famine, which caused the death of millions of people. In addition, Mao carried out the Cultural Revolution, a movement that had a massive impact on Chinese society and caused great instability.

Legacy and lasting impact:

Mao Zedong's legacy is complex and subject to debate. He is considered both a revolutionary and patriotic leader and a dictator and responsible for gross human rights violations. His regime had a lasting impact on China and world politics. Mao established a political system based on Maoism and laid the foundation for Chinese socialism. However, his leadership has also been the subject of criticism and controversy due to the excesses and negative consequences of some of his policies.

Genghis Khan

His real name was Temujin, he was a military leader and founder of the Mongol Empire in the 13th century. Below, I will provide you with information about his historical context and biography, some key influences on his life, his contributions and achievements, as well as his legacy and lasting impact.

Historical context and biography:

Genghis Khan was born in 1162 in the Mongolian steppes. At that time, the Mongol tribes were fragmented and in constant conflict. Genghis Khan succeeded in unifying the tribes under his leadership and established the Mongol Empire, which expanded from Central Asia to Eastern Europe and East Asia.

Intimate life and curious facts:

Specific information about Genghis Khan's intimate life is scarce. It is known that he had multiple wives and concubines, and he is credited with extensive offspring. However, exact details about his personal life and relationships are difficult to determine with precision.

Key influences and experiences in his life:

Genghis Khan was influenced by the nomadic culture and traditions of the Mongol steppes. He learned valuable leadership and strategic skills during his youth, and witnessed the conflicts and rivalries between tribes. These experiences led him to seek the unification of the Mongol tribes under his leadership.

Contributions and achievements that impacted the world:

Genghis Khan led a series of successful military campaigns that resulted in the creation of the vast Mongol Empire. His army was known for its speed, organization and innovative tactics. The empire established under his leadership became one of the largest in history, and his legacy spanned centuries.

Legacy and lasting impact:

Genghis Khan's legacy is complex. On the one hand, his empire promoted trade, communication and cultural exchange in Eurasia. In addition, he implemented policies that fostered peace and stability in the conquered regions. However, he is also credited with the destruction and violence associated with the conquests of the Mongol Empire.

On a cultural level, Genghis Khan's empire influenced the spread of Mongolian culture and the promotion of cultural exchanges through trade routes. In addition, its military and political impact laid the foundation for later empires in Eurasia.

It is important to keep in mind that Genghis Khan's conquests came at a significant human cost and caused devastation in many regions. However, his leadership and legacy have left a lasting imprint on world history and the way cultures interacted and developed in Eurasia.

Nikola Tesla

He was an inventor, electrical engineer and scientist of Serbian origin who lived in the 19th and early 20th century.

Historical context and biography:

Nikola Tesla was born on July 10, 1856 in the Austrian Empire, which today corresponds to modern Croatia. During his lifetime, he witnessed important scientific and technological breakthroughs, such as the invention of electricity and the expansion of the electrical industry.

Intimate life and curious facts:

Tesla devoted much of his life to his work and scientific research, so little is known about his intimate life. There are no known records of him having had a wife or a prominent love life. Tesla apparently led an austere life focused on his work.

Key influences and experiences in his life:

Tesla was influenced by inventors and scientists of his time, such as Thomas Edison and Heinrich Hertz. He also had a broad scientific and technical education, which allowed him to explore various areas of science and develop his own innovative approach to the field of electricity.

Contributions and achievements that impacted the world:

Tesla is known for his numerous contributions and inventions in the field of electricity and electrical engineering. Some of his most notable achievements include the development of alternating current (AC), the invention of the AC induction motor, and the construction of the first hydroelectric power plant at Niagara Falls. His inventions laid the foundation for the development of large-scale electric power generation and distribution systems.

Legacy and lasting impact:

Tesla's legacy is significant in the scientific and technological realm. His contributions to electricity and electrical engineering revolutionized the way electrical power was generated and transmitted, and laid the foundation for the development of modern industrial society. His emphasis on alternating current has been fundamental in the field of long-distance electrical power transmission.

Although Tesla did not have the recognition and financial success during his lifetime that other inventors of his time achieved, his legacy has been recognized and valued in the decades since his death. His name is associated with scientific genius and his work continues to inspire scientists, inventors and technologists around the world. The international electrical engineering award, the "Nikola Tesla Award," was established in his honor, and his name remains synonymous with innovation and progress in the electrical industry.

Bill Gates

Whose full name is William Henry Gates III, is an American entrepreneur, philanthropist and business magnate. Below, I will provide you with information about his historical context and biography, key influences in his life, contributions and achievements, as well as his legacy and lasting impact. However, please note that information about his intimate life may be limited due to the privacy of the individual:

Historical context and biography:

Bill Gates was born on October 28, 1955 in Seattle, Washington, USA. He grew up in a middle-class family and from an early age showed an interest in technology and computers. Gates attended Harvard University, where he met Paul Allen, with whom he would later co-found Microsoft.

Intimate life:

Bill Gates married Melinda French in 1994. They had three children together. However, in May 2021, they announced their divorce after 27 years of marriage.

Key influences and experiences in his life:

Gates was influenced by his passion for technology and programming from an early age. His meeting with Paul Allen at Harvard University was pivotal to his later collaboration in the creation of Microsoft. Gates was also influenced by his relationship with his mother, who encouraged him to follow his interests and pursue his dreams.

Contributions and achievements that impacted the world:

Bill Gates is known for being one of the founders of Microsoft, one of the most influential software companies in the world. Under his leadership, Microsoft developed the Windows operating system, which became one of the most widely used platforms for personal computers. Gates has also made significant contributions to philanthropy through the Bill and Melinda Gates Foundation, which is dedicated to addressing global issues such as poverty, health and education.

Bill Gates' legacy is significant in the technology industry and in the field of philanthropy. His entrepreneurial vision and leadership at Microsoft contributed to the advancement of personal computing and laid the foundation for the development of the modern technology industry. In addition, his focus on philanthropy has had a global impact on improving the health, education and living conditions of those most in need.

Gates is recognized as one of the world's most successful entrepreneurs and influential philanthropists. His focus on using technology and resources to address global challenges has left a lasting legacy and continues to inspire other business leaders and philanthropists to follow his example.

Plato

His real name was Aristocles, he was a Greek philosopher born around 427 BC in Athens, Greece. He is considered one of the most influential thinkers in Western history and one of the most prominent disciples of Socrates.

Not many specific details are known about Plato's intimate life and personal relationships, as the available historical information focuses mainly on his philosophical teachings and writings.

Curious facts about Plato include his participation in the Peloponnesian War and his close relationship with Socrates, whom he considered his teacher and whose death marked a significant impact on his life and philosophy.

Key influences and experiences in his life:

The main influence in Plato's life was his teacher Socrates, whose philosophical methods and approach to the search for truth had a profound impact on his thinking. Another important aspect of his life was his trip to Egypt, where it is believed that he came into contact with the teachings of the Egyptian priests and became familiar with the philosophy and sciences of that culture.

Contributions and achievements that impacted the world:

Plato founded the Academy of Athens, one of the most important educational institutions of antiquity, where numerous leading philosophers and thinkers were trained. His philosophical dialogues, written in the form of conversations between characters, explore a wide range of topics, such as ethics, politics, metaphysics and epistemology. His most famous work is "The Republic", where he presents his ideal vision of a just state and the theory of Ideas.

Legacy and lasting impact:

Plato's legacy lies in his philosophical approach and his contribution to the development of Western thought. His ideas about reality, morality and justice have had a lasting influence on philosophy, politics, theology and other disciplines. Moreover, his method of dialogue and his search for truth have been a source of inspiration for generations of thinkers and scholars.

Plato also laid the foundation for the systematic study of philosophy, establishing the importance of reason and critical analysis. His work has influenced numerous philosophers and thinkers throughout history, and its impact extends to the present day.

William Shakespeare

Considered one of the most influential writers in world literature, he lived in the 16th and 17th centuries, during the period known as the English Renaissance. He was born in Stratford-upon-Avon, England, in April 1564 and died on April 23, 1616.

As for his personal life, Shakespeare married Anne Hathaway in 1582, and they had three children together. Not many intimate details of his life are known, as the information available is limited. As for his sexual orientation, there are no conclusive records to indicate his sexual preference.

A curious fact about Shakespeare is that he is credited with theatrical works in various genres, such as tragedies, comedies, historical plays and sonnets. In addition, it is estimated that he contributed to the expansion of the English vocabulary, as he is credited with the creation of new words and phrases.

The key influences and experiences in Shakespeare's life are the subject of speculation, as no detailed biography is available. However, it is believed that he may have had access to a basic education in his youth and may have traveled to London to become involved in the world of theater and writing.

Shakespeare's contributions and achievements in literature and theater are enormous. He is the author of iconic plays such as "Romeo and Juliet," "Hamlet," "Macbeth," and "King Lear," among many others. His plays have been translated into numerous languages and are still performed in theaters around the world. Shakespeare revolutionized the theater of his time by introducing complex characters, elaborate plots and poetic language.

Shakespeare's legacy and lasting impact are undeniable. His plays continue to be studied and performed today, and his influence on literature, theater and culture is incalculable. His characters, such as Romeo, Juliet, Hamlet and Lady Macbeth, have become archetypes and iconic figures in the history of theater. Shakespeare is considered one of the most brilliant literary minds of all time and his legacy endures as an integral part of Western culture.

Alexander Graham Bell

Born on March 3, 1847 in Edinburgh, Scotland, and died on August 2, 1922 in Baddeck, Nova Scotia, he was a scientist, inventor and educator known primarily for inventing the telephone.

As for his personal life, Bell married Mabel Hubbard in 1877, with whom he had four children. Regarding his intimate life, not many details are available about his sex life, as it is not a widely documented aspect.

A curious fact about Bell is that, apart from his invention of the telephone, he was also involved in other fields, such as phonetics and aviation. He was a founding member of the National Geographic Society in 1888 and played a key role in the development of aviation, working on the design of airplanes and the improvement of aero engines.

Key influences and experiences in Alexander Graham Bell's life include his interest in communication and sound from an early age, as well as his work with speech and deafness. His mother and wife, both of whom were deaf, influenced his dedication to inventing devices that would help the hearing impaired.

Bell's most outstanding achievement was the invention of the telephone, patented in 1876. His work revolutionized long-distance communication, making it possible to transmit the human voice over wires. This invention had a significant impact on the world, transforming the way people communicated and opening up new possibilities for commerce, education and social relations.

Alexander Graham Bell's legacy is undeniable. In addition to the telephone, his contributions also include advances in areas such as telegraphy, aviation, education for the hearing impaired and sound technology. His work laid the foundation for the development of modern communications and his influence on technology and society endures to this day.

Joseph Stalin

(1878-1953) was a Soviet politician and leader who ruled the Soviet Union with an iron fist for much of the 20th century.

Historical context:

Stalin lived in an era marked by important historical events, such as the Russian Revolution of 1917 and World War II. He was born on December 18, 1878 in Gori, Georgia, which at that time was part of the Russian Empire. His life and political career unfolded in a period of intense social and political turmoil in Russia.

Biography:

Stalin was born Iosif Vissarionovich Dzhugashvili. He joined the Communist Party of the Soviet Union and became one of the outstanding leaders of the party. Stalin exercised authoritarian and totalitarian control over the country during his tenure as General Secretary of the party and later as leader of the Soviet Union.

Intimate life:

Stalin was married twice. His first wife, Ekaterina Svanidze, died in 1907. Later, he married Nadezhda Alliluyeva, with whom he had two children. However, their marital relationship was strained and Nadezhda committed suicide in 1932. Little is known about Stalin's intimate life, as he was a very private figure and his privacy was highly protected.

Curious facts:

Stalin adopted the surname "Stalin", meaning "man of steel", as a revolutionary name.

He was known for his ruthless personality and his ability to eliminate his political opponents through purges and executions.

Stalin was a heavy smoker and was often seen with a cigarette in his hand.

He had a fascination with movies and enjoyed Hollywood films.

Key influences and experiences:

Stalin was influenced by Marxist-Leninist thought, as well as by the October Revolution of 1917, in which he played an important role. In addition, his time in prison and his participation in revolutionary activities contributed to his political formation and his determination to achieve power.

Contributions and achievements:

He consolidated his power and established a totalitarian regime in the Soviet Union.

He implemented agrarian collectivization policies, which led to the elimination of private farms and the formation of collective farms.

He led the accelerated industrialization of the Soviet Union, transforming the country into an industrial power.

He played a key role in the victory of the Soviet Union in World War II and in the expansion of Soviet territory.

Cleopatra

(69 BC - 30 BC) was a queen of Egyptian origin who ruled ancient Egypt and played a crucial role in the events of the time. Below, I provide you with relevant information about her historical context, biography, personal life, influences, contributions and legacy:

Historical context:

Cleopatra lived during the Hellenistic period, a time when Egypt was under the influence of Macedonian-Greek culture and rule. During her reign, Egypt was under threat from the powerful Roman Empire and was engaged in internal struggles for control of the throne.

Biography:

Cleopatra was born in 69 BC in Alexandria, Egypt, and belonged to the Ptolemaic dynasty, a descendant of Ptolemy I, one of Alexander the Great's generals. She became queen at the age of 18 and reigned alongside her brother Ptolemy XIII. Throughout her life, Cleopatra had political and love affairs with prominent Roman leaders, such as Julius Caesar and Mark Antony.

Intimate life:

Cleopatra married her brother Ptolemy XIII, as was common in the Ptolemaic dynasty, but their relationship was strained and marked by power struggles. She had a lasting relationship with Julius Caesar, with whom she had a son named Caesarion. After Caesar's death, Cleopatra was united with Mark Antony and they had three children together. Cleopatra and Mark Antony committed suicide in 30 BC after their defeat by Octavian, the future emperor Augustus.

Curious facts:

Cleopatra spoke several languages, including Egyptian, Greek and Latin.

She was known for her beauty and her ability to seduce powerful men.

She is credited with using elaborate makeup techniques and perfumes to enhance her attractiveness.

Cleopatra was a shrewd politician and diplomat, and used her charm and skills to maintain power in a volatile political context.

Key influences and experiences:

Cleopatra was influenced by Greek culture and the legacy of Alexander the Great, as well as by the political and military tensions in the eastern Mediterranean. Her experiences included the struggle for the throne of Egypt, political alliances and her relationships with Roman leaders.

Contributions and achievements:

Cleopatra was a clever and astute ruler who maintained control of the Egyptian throne for several decades during a time of growing Roman influence.

He played a key role in the politics and diplomacy of his time, forging alliances and treaties to maintain Egypt's independence.

His relationship with influential Roman leaders, such as Julius Caesar and Mark Antony, allowed him to exert influence over political and military affairs in the world.

Karl Marx

He was a German philosopher, economist, sociologist and revolutionary, best known as the author of "The Communist Manifesto" and "Capital".

Historical context and biography:

Karl Marx was born on May 5, 1818 in Trier, in what is now Germany. He lived in a time of social change and upheaval, marked by the Industrial Revolution and the rise of capitalism. Marx became interested in philosophy, politics and economics from a young age, and became a fierce critic of the capitalist system and an advocate of socialism.

Wife and intimate life:

Marx married Jenny von Westphalen in 1843, and they had seven children together. Jenny was a loyal companion and actively supported Marx's intellectual work. Although the Marx family faced economic hardship for much of their lives, Jenny was a constant and supportive presence for Karl.

Curious facts:

Marx lived much of his life in exile due to his political activities. He spent several years in Paris and Brussels before settling in London, where he lived until his death in 1883. During his lifetime, Marx experienced financial difficulties and relied heavily on the financial support of his friend and collaborator, Friedrich Engels.

Key influences and experiences in his life:

Marx's ideas were influenced by philosophers such as Georg Wilhelm Friedrich Hegel and Ludwig Feuerbach, as well as by the labor and socialist movements of his time. He was also interested in the study of historical materialism and political economy, influencing his critical approach to capitalism and his vision of a communist society.

Contributions and achievements that impacted the world:

Marx is known for his theory of historical materialism and his critical analysis of capitalism. His works, such as "The Communist Manifesto" and "Das Kapital", have influenced political and economic thought, and have been fundamental to the development of the communist and socialist movement worldwide.

Legacy and lasting impact:

Marx's legacy has had a profound impact on politics, economics and society in general. His ideas have influenced numerous social and political movements throughout the 20th century and continue to be the subject of study and debate today. Marxism and scientific socialism based on his ideas have had a lasting impact in different countries and in the struggle for social justice, equality and the emancipation of workers.

As I mentioned earlier, Marx's legacy has been subject to interpretation and criticism over time. Some critics argue that his ideas led to totalitarian and repressive regimes in the 20th century, while others defend his vision of social equality and critique of the capitalist system.

Despite diverse interpretations, Marx's impact on political and economic theory has been undeniable. His analyses of the contradictions inherent in capitalism, such as the exploitation of workers and social inequalities, have led to important debates and have influenced the evolution of economics and social policies in many countries.

In addition, the Marxist approach has influenced sociology, anthropology and other fields of social science, helping to understand social dynamics, power relations and economic structures. His theoretical contributions have been the subject of study and critique by scholars and have inspired workers' movements, trade unions and struggles for social justice around the world. In short, Karl Marx left an intellectual and political legacy that has had a profound impact on economic, political and social theory.

Nicolaus Copernicus

(1473-1543) was a Polish astronomer and mathematician who formulated the heliocentric theory of the solar system, which revolutionized our understanding of the universe.

Historical context:

Copernicus lived in an era known as the Renaissance, a period of great scientific and cultural advances. He was born on February 19, 1473 in Thorn, Prussia, which at that time was part of the Kingdom of Poland. His work developed at a time of transition between the traditional geocentric conception of the universe and the scientific revolution to come.

Biography:

Copernicus studied mathematics and astronomy at the universities of Krakow, Bologna and Padua. Throughout his life, he worked as a clergyman, physician and administrator of ecclesiastical properties. He spent most of his life in the city of Frombork, Poland, where he conducted his astronomical research.

Intimate life:

Not much is known about Copernicus' personal life, as he was a private man. He neither married nor had children. As a Catholic clergyman, he was committed to celibacy.

Curious facts:

Copernicus was a polyglot and spoke several languages, including Polish, Latin, German, Italian and Greek.

In addition to his contributions to astronomy, he also studied medicine, economics and theology. Copernicus was a skilled musician and played the organ.

Key influences and experiences:

The main influences on Copernicus' life were the works of ancient Greek astronomers, such as Aristarchus of Samos, as well as the scientific advances and scholarly discussions of his time. The astronomical observations made by Copernicus and his interest in solving key mathematical and astronomical problems were fundamental to the development of his heliocentric theory.

Contributions and achievements:

Copernicus' main contribution was the formulation and publication of the heliocentric theory, which postulated that the Earth revolved around the Sun rather than being the center of the universe. His most famous work, "De revolutionibus orbium coelestium" ("On the Revolutions of the Celestial Spheres"), was published in 1543, shortly before his death.

His theory challenged the geocentric view of the universe and laid the foundations of modern astronomy by proposing a more accurate and coherent mathematical model.

Copernicus developed innovative mathematical methods and techniques for calculating the positions and motions of the planets, laying the foundation for the later development of calculus and celestial mechanics.

Christopher Columbus

His full name was Cristoforo Colombo, a Genoese navigator and explorer known for his transatlantic voyage in 1492, which resulted in Europe's discovery of America.

Historical context:

Christopher Columbus lived during the Renaissance, a period of great intellectual advances and scientific discoveries in Europe.

The historical context was marked by maritime expansion and the desire to find new trade routes to Asia.

Biography:

Columbus was born in Genoa, Italy, around 1451. He belonged to a merchant family.

He began his career as a sailor and gained experience in navigation and maritime trade.

Convinced that he could reach Asia by sailing westward, he sought financial support for his expedition and finally obtained the backing of the Catholic Monarchs of Spain.

In 1492, he set sail on his first transatlantic voyage and reached the Bahamas Islands, believing he had reached Asia.

He made several more trips to America, but never realized that he had discovered a whole new continent.

Wife, intimate life and curious facts:

Culón married Filipa Moniz Perestrelo in 1479, and they had a son named Diego.

Not many details are known about his intimate life or personal aspects beyond his career as an explorer, but it is said that he had a sweet tooth in the Americas, fornicating with the natives.

A curious fact is that Columbus took with him on his voyages a book entitled "Imago Mundi", written by the geographer Pierre d'Ailly, which influenced his beliefs about the shape and size of the Earth.

Contributions and achievements:

Columbus' main achievement was the discovery of America, which had a significant impact on world history by opening a new path to the American continent.

Although he initially believed he had reached Asia, his discovery paved the way for future European exploration and colonization in the Americas.

Columbus also contributed to the geographical and cartographic knowledge of the time, although his ideas about the shape of the Earth turned out to be wrong.

Legacy and lasting impact:

The legacy of Christopher Columbus is complex and controversial. Although he is recognized as an outstanding explorer, he is also criticized for the negative consequences of colonialism and the impact on the indigenous populations of the Americas.

Columbus' discovery of America marked the beginning of the Age of Discovery and changed world history by establishing lasting contact between Europe and America.

Columbus became a symbol and prominent figure in the history of Spain and an icon of exploration and discovery in general.